WIMBLEDON TO EPSOM

Vic Mitchell and Keith Smith

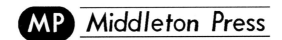
MP Middleton Press

*Cover picture: An up train from Sutton approaches Wimbledon on 2nd March 1957, while "Merchant Navy" class no. 35027 **Port Line** speeds west with a train for Bournemouth West. (R.C.Riley)*

First published November 1995

ISBN 1 873793 62 6

© Middleton Press 1995

Design - Deborah Goodridge

Published by Middleton Press
Easebourne Lane
Midhurst
West Sussex
GU29 9AZ
Tel: 01730 813169
Fax: 01730 812601

Printed & bound by Biddles Ltd,
Guildford and Kings Lynn

CONTENTS

ACKNOWLEDGEMENTS

We are very grateful for the help received from so many of those mentioned in the credits and also from P.G.Barnes, C.L.Caddy, R.M.Casserley, G.Croughton, M.Furnell, A.Ll.Lambert, N.Langridge, Mr.D. & Dr.S. Salter, G.T.V.Stacey, C.S.Watts and our ever helpful wives. We also thank Mrs. M.Mason and D.Wallis for permission to use the photograph by the late E.Wallis.

Route map of 1955

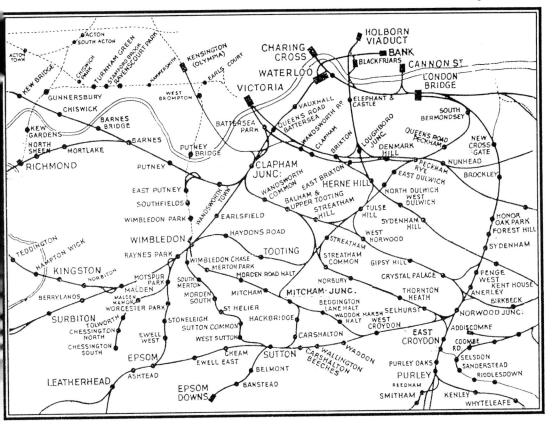

GEOGRAPHICAL SETTING

Both lines are almost entirely on London Clay and are situated between two Thames tributaries, the River Wandle and the Hogsmill River. Both routes cross the latter, its source being in Ewell. Epsom is about 150ft above sea level and its town centre is on the northern limit of the chalk of the dip slope of the North Downs. Ewell is similarly situated. The Epsom line south of Worcester Park is in Surrey, all the remainder now being in Greater London. The maps are to the scale of 25 ins to 1 mile, unless otherwise indicated.

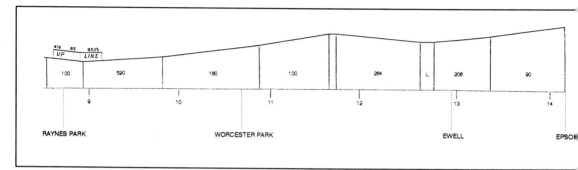

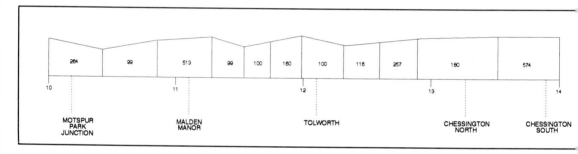

HISTORICAL BACKGROUND

The London & Southampton Railway was opened through Wimbledon on 21st May 1838 and became part of the London & South Western Railway in 1839. A branch from this line to Epsom was opened by the LSWR on 4th April 1859.

Meanwhile the London, Brighton & South Coast Railway had opened its line from West Croydon to Epsom on 10th May 1847. The route south to Leatherhead came into use in 1859 and was worked jointly by the two companies. They became constituents of the Southern Railway in 1923 and electrification of the Raynes Park - Epsom section took place on 12th July 1925, the line through Wimbledon having been energised in 1916.

The SR obtained an Act of Parliament in 1930 for the construction of a railway from Motspur Park to Leatherhead via Chessington. Rapid housing development was taking place in the northern part of the area but, owing to difficulties in purchasing land from speculators, work did not commence until 1936. The first section to Tolworth opened on 15th May 1938 and the length to Chessington South followed on 14th May 1939 (public services started two weeks after each of these dates).

The advent of World War II delayed completion of the scheme and the subsequent Green Belt legislation meant that the forecast residential expansion could not take place. Thus the line remains a branch to this day.

SOUTHERN RAILWAY.
This ticket is issued subject to the Company's Bye-laws, Regulations & Conditions in their Time Tables, Notices and Book of Regulations.
Raynes Park to
Raynes Park   Raynes Park
Wimbledon   Wimbledon
WIMBLEDON
Third Class (S.23) Third Class
Fare 2d   Fare 2d
2222

BRITISH RAILWAYS (S)
This ticket is issued subject to the Bye-laws, Regulations and Conditions contained in the Publications and Notices of and applicable to the Railway Executive.
Motspur Park to
Motspur Park   Motspur Park
Ashtead   Ashtead
ASHTEAD
THIRD CLASS   THIRD CLASS
Fare 1/1H   Fare 1/1H
NOT TRANSFERABLE
1903

2nd - SINGLE   SINGLE - 2nd
Wimbledon To
Wimbledon   Wimbledon
(S.2)   (S.2)
Chessington N'th or South   Chessington N'th or South
Hinchley Wood or   Hinchley Wood or
Thames Ditton   Thames Ditton
CHESSINGTON NORTH or SOUTH
HINCHLEY WOOD
or THAMES DITTON
Via Raynes Park
(S)   1/2   FARE   1/2   (S)
For condit'ns see over   For condit'ns see over
1056

PASSENGER SERVICES

The weekday timetable showed 10 trains in 1870 increasing to 14 in 1890 and 23 in 1910. There were four Sunday trains in the first two timetables and seven in the last.

The final steam operated service comprised a basic hourly service to Horsley on the Guildford line, giving 23 trains (including peak hour extras) on weekdays and 11 on Sundays.

Electrification in 1925 brought three trains per hour on weekdays. The two an hour on Sundays were soon increased to three. Opening to Tolworth and extension to Chessington South brought an additional three trains per hour, daily, to Motspur Park and stations to Waterloo.

Apart from wartime restrictions, these services were maintained on weekdays until reduced to 30 minute intervals on the Chessington branch on 15th September 1958 and similarly on the Epsom route on 17th June 1963.

On 28th May 1995, an additional Monday to Friday hourly train was introduced, this running non-stop between Wimbledon and Epsom and terminating at Guildford. On Saturdays, this fast train ran to Horsham. The Sunday timetable was half-hourly on the through route and on the branch, the latter having been reduced to hourly for a period from 1976.

Fares.] LEATHERHEAD, EPSOM, WIMBLEDON, and LONDON.—London & South Western.

Bradshaw February 1890

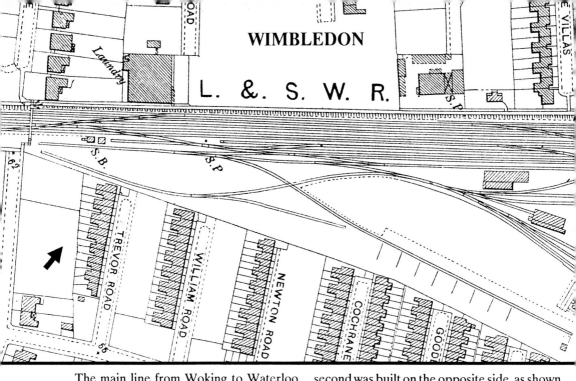

The main line from Woking to Waterloo runs from left to right. The first station was situated to the left of the road bridge; the second was built on the opposite side, as shown on this 1898 map. The LBSCR route from West Croydon is at the bottom.

1. On the left of this northward view is the LSWR's single up platform and the footbridge and steps to their down island platform. The footbridge on the right is part of the LBSCR station. (Lens of Sutton)

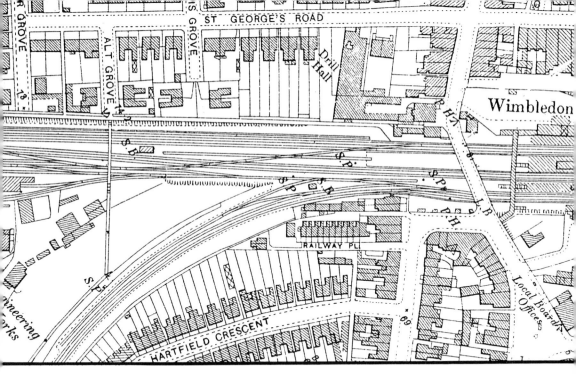

2. The LSWR opened a new station on the east side of the road bridge in the 1880s. The main building was on the north side of the line and is seen here, along with the footbridge marked on the map. The Putney line terminus is in the left background. (Pamlin Prints)

3. The ivy-clad house for the LBSCR station master is on the right, the driveway to that company's station being adjacent to it. On the left is the penny bazaar of Marks & Spencer. There is also aerial evidence of the electric tramway. (G.Gundry coll)

Diagram of the layout after the 1928 reconstruction (Railway Engineer)

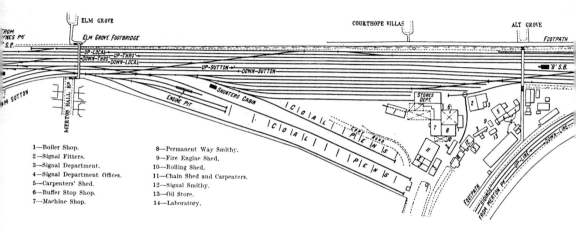

1—Boiler Shop.
2—Signal Fitters.
3—Signal Department.
4—Signal Department Offices.
5—Carpenters' Shed.
6—Buffer Stop Shop.
7—Machine Shop.

8—Permanent Way Smithy.
9—Fire Engine Shed.
10—Rolling Shed.
11—Chain Shed and Carpenters.
12—Signal Smithy.
13—Oil Store.
14—Laboratory.

4. Seen by the signal box at the west end of the map on 11th March 1922 is class 0278 0-6-0 no.273-A, built for the LSWR by Beyer Peacock in 1878. The box was designated "E" and was closed and demolished in 1929 to make way for the new line to Sutton, which was opened as far as South Merton on 7th July of that year. (H.C.Casserley)

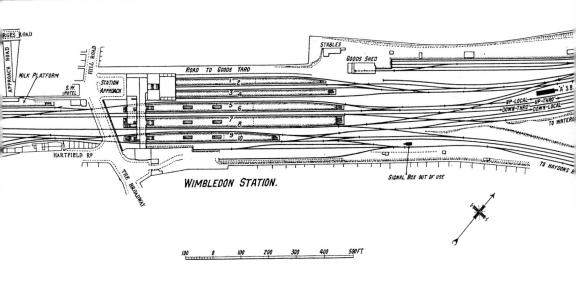

WIMBLEDON STATION.

5. Prior to the complete rebuilding of the station in 1927-28, the road bridge was widened. On the left are the entrances to the former District Railway and LSWR stations, while the driveway to the ex-LBSCR entrance appears white, top centre. The platforms on the right were removed. (Lens of Sutton)

6. West Yard is on the left as class L12 4-4-0 no.416 approaches the station on 21st June 1924. The platform on the right was designated for horse and carriage traffic at that time, it having an end loading dock near the road bridge. It was also known as "Volunteers Platform" due to it having been used in connection with military movements on Wimbledon Common. (H.C.Casserley)

7. Class 0395 0-6-0 no.0441 of 1883 shunts West Yard on 12th May 1927. Built by Neilsons, this locomotive survived to become BR no.30577. The connection across the main lines was shortened later that year. (H.C.Casserley)

8. The old urinal stood defiantly on Sunday 19th February 1928 as the new canopy framework was being erected. The former LBSCR tracks in the foreground were still devoid of conductor rails. (H.C.Casserley)

9. Wimbledon "D" box (64 levers) was photographed on the same day when it was about to be moved 12 ft to the right. Using trolleys and hand worked winches, the journey took 17 minutes. It became "B" box five weeks later, when the number of boxes at Wimbledon was reduced from five to three. The milk dock is in the background and was completed in 1926. (H.C.Casserley)

10. A class Q1 is in the distance as a Holborn Viaduct to West Croydon train runs through past West Yard in 1956. The coaches, which had wooden framed bodies, were formed as three-car units until the late 1940s when a wider all-steel vehicle was added. (F.Hornby)

11. Class Q1 0-6-0 no.33008 approaches the reverse curves on the up local line on 2nd March 1957, while a train on the up main passes under the bridge. Headcode 12 indicates that 2BIL no.2034 is heading for Alton. The vans are in the milk dock. (R.C.Riley)

12. All steel 4 SUBs, with improved impact strength and fire resistance, formed the second generation of electric stock on the route. No.4640 was photographed on 9th June 1957, bound for Chessington South. The ferry vans in the background conveyed motor scooters imported from Italy to the former milk dock. The footbridge behind its roof was built in 1926 to carry a footpath above the milk lorries. (N.L.Browne)

13. "Lord Nelson" class no.30855 *Robert Blake* leaves West Yard with 2-HAP sets nos. 5613, 6008 and 2 BIL unit no. 2096 en route for Eastleigh Works. Beyond, class C2X 0-6-0 no.32546 stands ready to leave with a goods for Norwood Junction via Mitcham while class Q1 no.33038 waits to resume yard shunting on 10th January 1959. (J.N.Faulkner)

14. On 2nd and 16th December 1962, the SLS and RCTS ran a railtour to include the Shepperton, Hampton Court and Chessington branches. Having run on the up main line, Beattie Well Tanks nos.30585 and 30587 propel the train onto the down goods loop, which extended as far as Raynes Park. The train is seen later in picture nos.32 and 47. The Sutton lines, "C" box and West Yard shunting neck are behind the train. (S.C.Nash)

15. Electric locomotive no. 20001 (formerly no.CC1) was recorded on the down main line on 3rd June 1964 hauling a "Derby Day" special to Epsom for the Sudanese Suite. Behind it is "A" box which was in use from 22nd February 1948 until 12th April 1990, although it continued to control the East Putney line until 25th February 1991. (J.Scrace)

16. No.73139 sets back into West Yard with a coal train from Acton Yard, destined for the two concentration depots on the Chessington branch on 28th May 1974. At this time, unbraked wagons were still in use, requiring the provision of two brake tenders for the journey via the West London line and Tooting. General goods facilities had been withdrawn here on 5th January 1970. (J.N.Faulkner)

0014
SOUTHERN RAILWAY
Available on Day of issue only
Crystal Palace (L L) to
WORCESTER PARK
Third Class Including
Admission to the PALACE
FOR CONDITIONS
SEE BACK
SOUTHERN RAILWAY
Available on Day of issue only
Worcester Park to
CRYSTAL PAL'CE (L L)
Third Class (L.A.)
0014

1998
SOUTHERN RAILWAY.
Issued subject to the Bye-laws
Regulations & Conditions in the
Company's Bills and Notices.
H.M.F. on LEAVE.
Blackfriars Holborn V.
Victoria or Waterloo to
CHESSINGTON NORTH
Third Class
NOT TRANSFERABLE
SOUTHERN RAILWAY.
H.M.F. on LEAVE
Chessington North to
BLACKFRIARS
HOLBORN VIADUCT.
VICTORIA or WATERLOO
Third Class.
1998

17. The new "C" Box opened on 28th April 1929 in readiness for the opening of the route to Sutton. It also controlled access to the down goods loop, which had been in use since 1900. The brick wall was built during World War II to give blast protection to the vital entrails of the box, which closed on 16th April 1990. (J.Scrace)

Companion albums to feature this station -
Waterloo to Woking (1986)
Mitcham Junction Lines (1992)
Lines around Wimbledon (1996)
and *Kingston and Wimbledon Tramways* (1995)

18. Having called at West Yard to attach vans on 8th December 1987, no.58023 has run on to the down local line on its way to the Chessington branch with a load of coal. The new Waterloo Area Signalling Centre was built in West Yard to eventually control the routes out to Berrylands and Leatherhead. The first phase of WARS - Waterloo Area Resignalling Scheme - was commissioned on 5th February 1984. (J.S.Petley)

19. The shops seen on the bridge in the background on picture no.11 were replaced in 1991 by much larger retail premises, resulting in the creation of a lengthy tunnel. Class 455 no.5847 is on the down local line on 21st February 1992, working the 15.16 Waterloo to Guildford service via Claygate. (V.Mitchell)

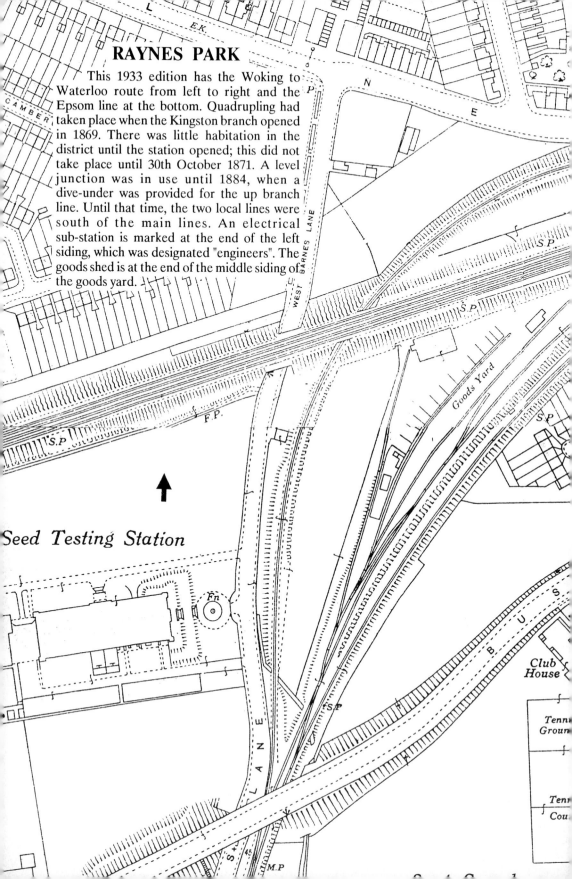

RAYNES PARK

This 1933 edition has the Woking to Waterloo route from left to right and the Epsom line at the bottom. Quadrupling had taken place when the Kingston branch opened in 1869. There was little habitation in the district until the station opened; this did not take place until 30th October 1871. A level junction was in use until 1884, when a dive-under was provided for the up branch line. Until that time, the two local lines were south of the main lines. An electrical sub-station is marked at the end of the left siding, which was designated "engineers". The goods shed is at the end of the middle siding of the goods yard.

Seed Testing Station

Goods Yard

Club House

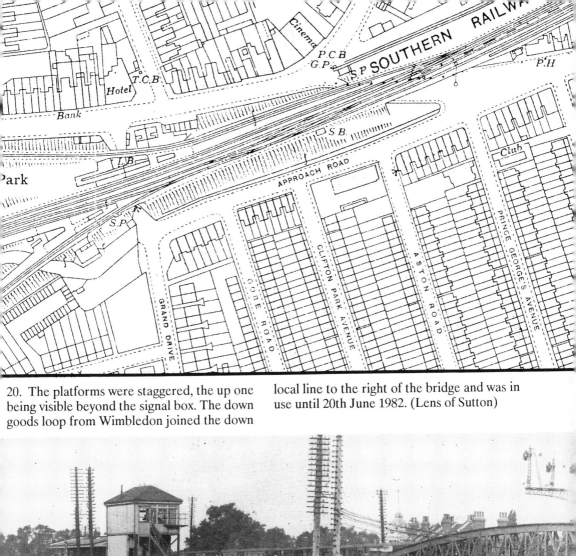

20. The platforms were staggered, the up one being visible beyond the signal box. The down goods loop from Wimbledon joined the down local line to the right of the bridge and was in use until 20th June 1982. (Lens of Sutton)

RAYNES PARK, – THE RAILWAY STATION.

21. Cottages and a modest building were provided on the up side. The standards and overhead equipment were on the London United Tramway's route to Hampton Court, which provided competition for the railway from 1907. (Lens of Sutton)

SOUTHERN RAILWAY.
Issued subject to the Bye-laws, Regulations &
Conditions in the Company's Bills and Notices.
342
Motspur Park to
Motspur Park
Raynes Park
Motspur Park
Raynes Park
RAYNES PARK 342
THIRD CLASS
Fare 2½d.
THIRD CLASS
Fare 2½d.
NOT TRANSFERABLE.

7557 CHILD
2nd-SINGLE
Raynes Park to
WIMBLEDON
(S) 2d. FARE 2d. (S)
FOR CONDITIONS SEE OVER
CHILD 7557

22. The down platform for Epsom trains is curved and on a falling gradient of 1 in 100. The canopy on the left is on the down local line. (Lens of Sutton)

23. Class T14 no.443 approaches Raynes Park with a Templecombe to Wimbledon milk train on 9th August 1919. This would decant a vast number of milk churns on to the passenger platform at Wimbledon on arrival. (K.Nunn/LCGB)

24. The up platform is seen in October 1933; the up branch trains called at the far side of it. A sand drag was added in 1935 to prevent such trains running through the points on to the up local line. (Lens of Sutton)

25. No. 34058 *Sir Frederick Pile* transfers a down West of England express to the up main line over a temporary crossover during bridge rebuilding at Malden on 20th September 1959. Beyond the hand signalman is the signal box which was in use until 5th May 1990. (J.H.Aston)

26. Viewed from the end of the footbridge on 29th March 1963 is class 5 no.73065 with empty coal wagons from Tolworth Coal Concentration Depot. (J.Scrace)

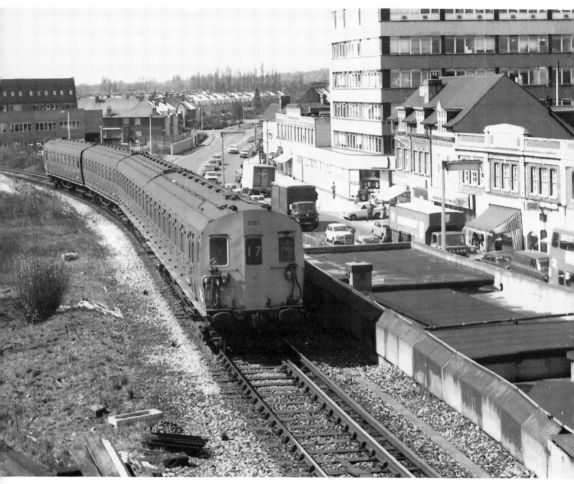

27. A view from the same location on 11th April 1978 reveals the extent of business development in the area and more of the flat roof of the 1935 station buildings. Unit no.5131 is working the 12.41 Dorking to Waterloo. (J.Scrace)

0048

SOUTHERN RAILWAY
MONTHLY RETURN
Available as advertised
Southwold to
EPSOM

Via Eastern Counties Omnibus,
Halesworth, L. & N. E. Rly.,
Liverpool St. & London (S.R)
Third Class Fare 21/-

FOR CONDITIONS
SEE BACK.

SOUTHERN RAILWAY.
MONTHLY RETURN
Available as advertised
Epsom to
SOUTHWOLD

Via London (S.R.), Liverpool St,
L. & N. E. Rly., Halesworth &
Eastern Counties Omnibus
Third Class Fare 21/-

0048

28. During April 1995, the bridge carrying the quadruple track over the up branch line was replaced and from the 8th to the 18th trains to Epsom and beyond started at Raynes Park, platform 4. A connection for Chessington South was provided at Motspur Park. The new concrete bridge beams were thicker than their predecessors and so the trackbed of the line underneath had to be lowered. The sub station is in the background but the electrical control room for the area is obscured by the crane. (British Rail)

29. The bridge on the right carries Bushey Road, which was built to link Kingston Road with the Kingston Bypass. Trams between Wimbledon and Hampton Court were replaced by trolleybuses in 1931, one of the first such conversions in the London area These early vehicles were known as "Diddlers". The middle track is to the goods yard, which closed on 4th December 1967. (E.Johnson coll)

30. The 16.12 Waterloo to Effingham Junction was operated by unit no.5114 on 6th April 1978. It is running under Bushey Road bridge and is passing Raynes Park goods ground frame. This box was known as Raynes Crossing (no Park) until 12th December 1965, when the level crossing it controlled was reduced to a footpath. (J.Scrace)

31. An earlier picture of the box reveals the minor nature of the road crossing. The crossing keeper's cottage and hut would predate the box. The tramway standard carries a request stop sign- "Electric cars stop here if required". (Lens of Sutton)

32. The same box is seen again as class H16 4-6-2T no.30517 heads south with the train seen earlier in picture no.14. The buffers of the goods yard head shunt are visible under the bridge. The crossover was taken out of use on 13th November 1985. (R.C.Riley)

33. Further south is West Barnes Lane Crossing which was fitted with barriers controlled from the gate box. CCTV was installed in June 1978 so that they could be worked from Raynes Park box. (J.Scrace)

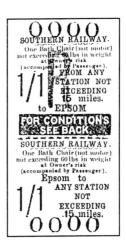

MOTSPUR PARK

34. The meandering West Barnes Lane crosses the route again further south, at Blue House Crossing. A cottage, box and hut were provided, the latter being in brick. The box was renamed Motspur Park on 23rd September 1929. We look east prior to the postcard being franked in 1908. (G.Gundry coll)

35. Initially, access to the island platform was only possible from the down side. Note the short canopy provided in the early years. (Lens of Sutton)

0560 CHILD 3rd·SINGLE CHILD 0560
Motspur Park to
RAYNES PARK
(8) 2d H FARE 2d H (8)
For Conditions see over

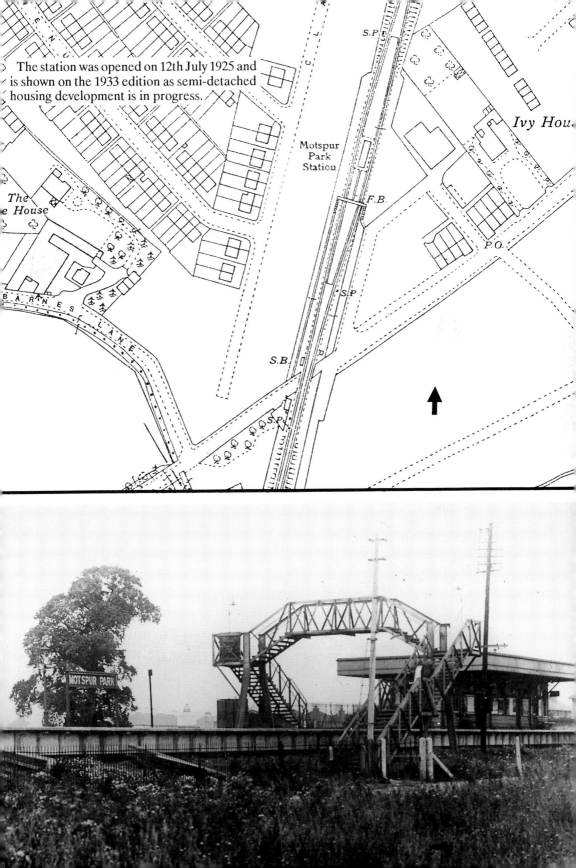

The station was opened on 12th July 1925 and is shown on the 1933 edition as semi-detached housing development is in progress.

Motspur Park Station

Ivy Hou.

The House

BARNES LANE

S.P.

S.P.

F.B.

S.P.

P.O.

S.P.

S.B.

MOTSPUR PARK

36. The canopy was extended in June 1938 and a footbridge over the up line was added. Lattice signal posts were widely favoured by the LSWR but were replaced by the SR with ones built from two running rails. (D.Cullum coll)

37. Relaying of the down line is viewed from the platform on 2nd October 1955. No total closures in those days - a Waterloo to Dorking 4 SUB is working "wrong line" to maintain the service. (J.N.Faulkner)

38. The box worked the junction of the Chessington branch electrically and was photographed in 1967. It controlled the whole of the branch from 29th January 1972 until 21st July 1990, when WARS stage 7 was completed and the box became redundant. (J.Scrace)

39. A southwards panorama from the footbridge on 2nd April 1995 includes the 12.50 Waterloo to Chessington South and the CCTV cameras which convey images to the new signalling centre at Wimbledon. Controlled barriers had been brought into use on 3rd November 1974. (M.J.Stretton)

Chessington Branch
MALDEN MANOR

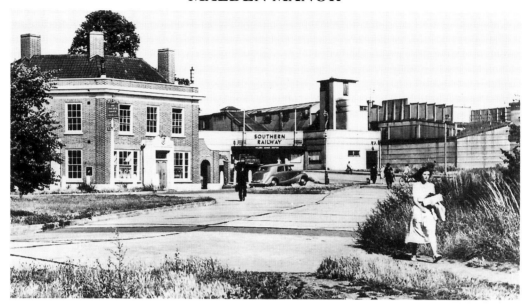

40. The monotony of concrete roads, concrete fences, concrete walls and a concrete station was relieved by the brick-built public house, "The Malden Manor". Opened with the line to Tolworth on 28th May 1938, the railway architecture was similar to the other stations on the branch. (Lens of Sutton)

41. Known as Chisarc cantilevers, the canopy supports gave a completely clear platform surface. These stations were among the first to have fluorescent tube lights, the uniformity being broken by the use of different colour tubes. This is a lesson that could be learnt to advantage by today's railway managers. (British Rail)

42. Photographed in the 1970s, the station appears to have a goods lift. While the shafts were built, at all the stations on the branch, they were never fitted with mechanisms, a 1 in 10 ramp being provided as a cheaper alternative in most cases. (British Rail)

43. Houses stretch into the distance as the 12.37 from Chessington South arrives on 2nd April 1995. The concrete bridges were another illusion. The steel girders were coated with the material in the belief that they would be protected. (M.J.Stretton)

44. The undulating landform necessitated numerous embankments but rather fewer cuttings. The former were largely built with rubble from London slum clearance. This northward view includes two sidings but no housing. (R.Shepherd)

45. The contractors provided the usual variety of equipment and made a base at Tolworth. The deep cutting at Chessington was their greatest challenge. Large quantities of ash and hardcore were laid and rolled on the floor before the Meldon track ballast was spread. There were nine bridges to build, plus a 140ft long viaduct over the Hogsmill River. (R.Shepherd)

46. An up train has just departed and is accelerating on a 1 in 100 down gradient as we gaze at the smooth curves of the canopies. How great is the contrast with the angular form of the 20-lever signal box, which was presumably designed in a different department. (Lens of Sutton)

47. Three of Tolworth's five sidings are evident as the RCTS/SLS railtour (seen in pictures 14 and 32) runs south. One report states that the number of sidings was increased from four to seven in 1940 to give wartime storage for Pullman cars. (D.Trevor Rowe)

48. Class Q1 0-6-0 no. 33001 arrives with coal for the nearby depot on 30th April 1963. The first of its class, it was selected for preservation by the National Railway Museum and is now on loan to the Bluebell Railway. (J.N.Faulkner)

49. The SR referred to the style as "Marine", seemingly related to the "Cunarder" concept. By the time that it was pictured in the 1970s, "Odeon" was the popular term, a word once well known in the cinema world. "Art deco" is the formal term. (British Rail)

50. Standing in the goods yard on 25th May 1963 is class S15 4-6-0 no. 30839. On the left is the station and signal box on the embankment. Also evident are the then new coal pens of concrete block construction. The yard ceased to handle general goods on 3rd May 1965 and subsequently specialised in coal. (A.N.Davenport)

51. A coal train stands on the shunting neck on 5th January 1967 as class 3 no. 77014 runs south with the "South Western Suburban" railtour. Having come from Waterloo via East Putney, it returned via Shepperton, Windsor & Eton, Reading Central Goods, Ascot, Virginia Water, Surbiton and Hampton Court! (J.Scrace)

52. Work started in October 1970 to equip the yard with mechanised coal handling equipment. The two southern sidings were removed and the National Coal Board provided its own Barclay diesel for shunting. It was recorded on 21st July 1971. (R.E.Ruffell)

53. A freshly painted class 04 diesel was pictured on 2nd April 1974 in front of the coal conveyer and bins. A large proportion of the local houses were heated by solid fuel at that time, necessitating up to 17 coal trains per week to this depot. (R.E.Ruffell)

54. The depot is seen from the down platform on 8th July 1989, the year in which the NCB ceased to use it. Marine aggregates from Newhaven were unloaded here by that time. The crossover had been added in 1970. (A.N.Davenport)

55. A closer view of the conveyer on 9th February 1993 shows the bogies on which its outer end travelled on an arc of track. Wagons containing different products discharged into a pit under the locomotive and the belt could be positioned to load the appropriate bin. (M.J.Stretton)

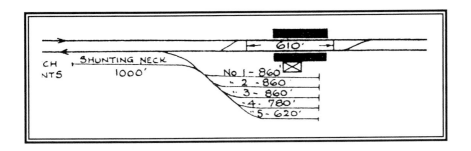

56. Class 455 no. 5722 passes the yard connections while working an up service on the same day. These had been controlled by a 12-lever ground frame since 16th January 1972. The signal box closed two weeks later. (M.J.Stretton)

CHESSINGTON NORTH

57. Until shortly before opening, the plan had been to name this station "Chessington Court" and its southerly neighbour "Chessington Grange". The change of plan did nothing to help passengers find the zoo, particularly as it is advertised on this platform. Car stops 3, 6 and 8 are marked. (Lens of Sutton)

58. Built only one year after Tolworth, it is surprising that the elegant curves were abandoned; compare this picture with no. 46. Class 415 (4EPB) no. 5127 stands at the down platform on 2nd October 1983. Class 455 units were introduced to the line that year. (F.Hornby)

59. Unlike the 1938 stations, the two final ones were finished with red brick. The entrance is on the up side and is seen in April 1995. Island platforms had been proposed for the branch but large projected traffic figures meant that the stations would not be like those on the 1929 Wimbledon-Sutton line. (M.J.Stretton)

0007
SOUTHERN RAILWAY
Issued subject to the Bye-laws,
Regulations & Conditions in the
Company's Bills & Notices
Daily Express Air
Pageant as advertised
Gatwick Airport to
CHESSINGTON NORTH
Third Class
10th. JULY 1948.
NOT TRANSFERABLE.
- - - - - - - - - -
SOUTHERN RAILWAY
Daily Express Air
Pageant, as advertised
Chessington North to
GATWICK AIRPORT
Third Class
10th JULY 1948.
0007

CHESSINGTON SOUTH

60. Although both platforms were completed, only the down one was ever used. The up side was used for berthing purposes. In the background is the electrical sub-station, which was also built of concrete. Also evident are government offices which generated extra traffic here. (Lens of Sutton)

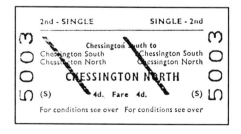

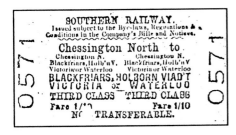

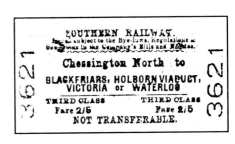

61. Chessington Zoo provided a novel form of transport between their premises and the station from 1944-49. The bus subsequently went to the USA, having originally been used in London by the Star Omnibus Company, a Cardiff firm in business in 1899-1908. The vehicle was repatriated in 1988 and is now in the Welsh Industrial and Maritime Museum. (H.C.Casserley coll.)

62. H.M. The Queen normally returns to London from Epsom Races by road but on 2nd June 1954 her party was provided with four Pullman cars and no. 34011 *Tavistock*. Royal down trains always use Tattenham Corner station. "OFF" was an order to guards regarding 4 SUB train heating. (B.Morrison)

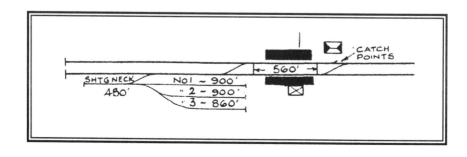

63. The 08.35 departure for Waterloo on 8th October 1970 was formed of two 4 SUB units. The leading one is formed of HAL/SUB/SUB/HAL vehicles. The 18-lever signal box (left) was in use until 30th January 1972. EPB units appeared at weekends in the mid-1970s. (R.E.Ruffell)

64. Class 508 units were introduced to the route in 1980, this example being recorded on 25th March of that year. Tightlock couplings were then a new concept in the area. After three years, the fleet moved to the Wirral. (R.E.Ruffell)

65. The Southern Electric Group ran a rail-tour on 17th March 1984 using electro-diesel no. 73126 and two 4TC units. The units had a driving compartment at each end, which meant that the locomotive could propel the train back. (F.Hornby)

The plan has been reduced to 2.25mm to 1ft and includes the ends of the three sidings in the goods yard. This closed to general traffic on 18th March 1963, having opened on 1st July 1939.

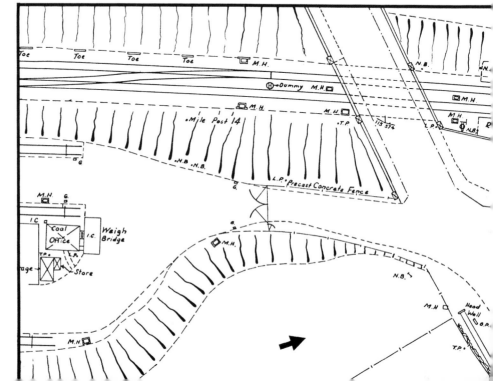

66. This was the only station on the branch to have the booking office at a higher level than the platforms but from 1971 an office was provided on the platform. The 08.50 is waiting to depart on 2nd April 1995. By this time the zoo had become the *World of Adventures* offering the public a crazy Toytown, Calamity Canyon, Rameses Revenge and a Seastorm. An entertaining link with the railway station is awaited as the post-motor car age approaches. (M.J.Stretton)

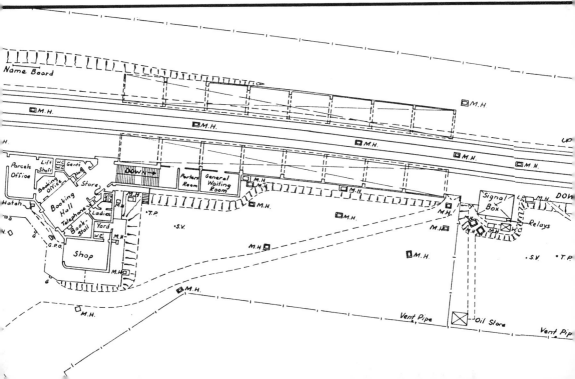

67. A southward view in 1994 shows part of the incomplete route to Leatherhead. There were 33 chains of track, 20 of which were once electrified. A further embankment was built during World War II as an exercise by the Royal Engineers, using spoil from sites where emergency spurs were being laid. (A.N.Davenport)

68. Charringtons opened a Coal Concentration Depot in May 1963, using two of the three sidings. Coal drops were built and a capstan and rope provided to move wagons over them. There were up to seven trains per week in the 1970s but traffic declined and ceased at the end of the 1980s. Arrival was timed at 03.21 and departure was 04.20, so no photographs exist of coal trains here. (M.Turvey)

CHESSINGTON ZOO

69. Barnard & Company of Norwich supplied *Queen Elizabeth* and *Oliver Cromwell* in 1937-38. The latter is seen in 1943, by then renamed *Princess Elizabeth* (it was later *Queen Elizabeth*) the former became *Princess Margaret*. Owing to a shortage of petrol for the locomotive's Austin 10 engine, a bag was fitted to carry coal gas. Your author (VM) is sitting nearest to the flexible gas pipes. The gauge was later doubled to 2ft, the line closing in 1978. (Mrs A.H.Mitchell)

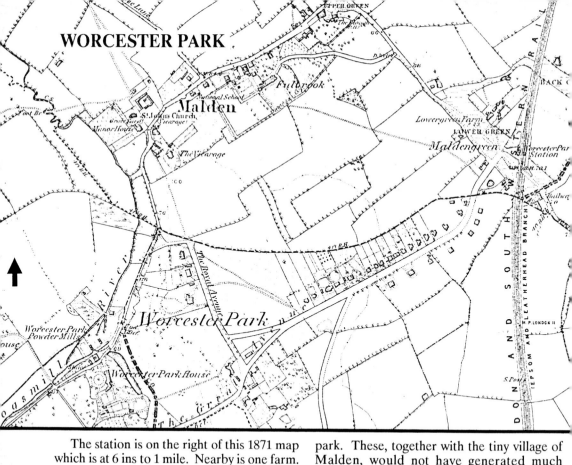

WORCESTER PARK

The station is on the right of this 1871 map which is at 6 ins to 1 mile. Nearby is one farm. A few spacious houses separate it from the park. These, together with the tiny village of Malden, would not have generated much traffic.

70. A northward view from the footbridge includes the two-tone paintwork beloved by the LSWR. The valence is picked out in salmon pink and brown, as were the company's passenger coaches. The station opened with the line and was "Old Malden and Worcester Park" until February 1862. The crossover was moved further north in October 1935. (Lens of Sutton)

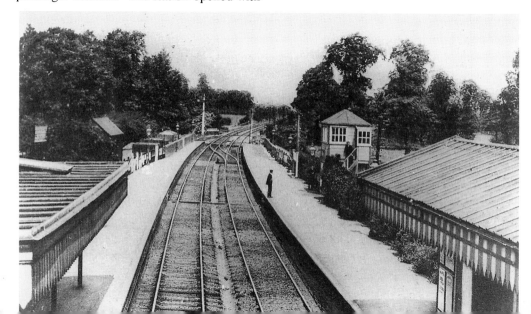

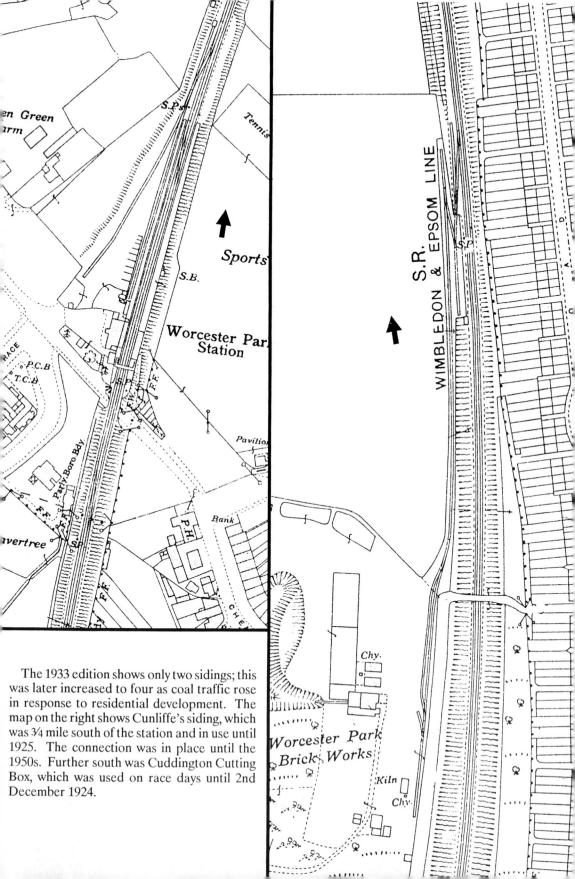

en Green
arm

S.P.s.

Tennis

Sports

S.B.

Worcester Park
Station

RACE

P.C.B.

T.C.B.

S.P.
F.F.
F.W.

Party Boro Bdy

Pavilion

Bank

F.F.

F.F.
S.P.

vertree

P.H.

CHE

F.F.

S.R. & EPSOM LINE

WIMBLEDON

S.P.

Chy.

Worcester Park
Brick Works

Kiln

Chy.

The 1933 edition shows only two sidings; this was later increased to four as coal traffic rose in response to residential development. The map on the right shows Cunliffe's siding, which was ¾ mile south of the station and in use until 1925. The connection was in place until the 1950s. Further south was Cuddington Cutting Box, which was used on race days until 2nd December 1924.

71. The road from Cheam passes under the bridge on the right and runs past the wide station approach in front of which the photographer seems to have parked his car. (Lens of Sutton)

72. A down train departs as some passengers cross the footbridge and others emerge from the footway that leads down from the platform to the highway. (Lens of Sutton)

73. Without the benefit of the nameboard on the left, it would be difficult to distinguish this station from other LSWR stations, so numerous are that company's characteristic features. (Lens of Sutton)

74. With conductor rails ready for regular use, class M7 no. E129 runs in with the 6.35pm Waterloo to Horsley on 1st June 1925. This termination point is featured in our *Branch Lines to Effingham Junction*. The signal box was in use until 27th February 1966. (H.C.Casserley)

0288
SOUTHERN RAILWAY.
Stoneleigh to
MALDEN MANOR
Third Class Fare 11d
FOR CONDITIONS
SEE BACK
SOUTHERN RAILWAY.
Malden Manor
Stoneleigh

Malden Manor to
STONELEIGH
Third Class Fare 11d

0288

20410
BRITISH RAIL (S)
2nd - OFF PEAK RETURN
WORCESTER
FARE 001 PARK
(5579B) to
CLAPHAM JCT
VALID
as dated
By
authorised trains
AND BACK
For conditions
enquire ticket office
NOT TRANSFERABLE
- 7 NOV 87

76. The bridge over the B283 (now A2043) Malden Road was rebuilt to increase head-room and road width. This and the following two photographs were taken on 4th November 1962. (A.N.Davenport)

75. The deep eaves and round-head windows were lost in favour of the SR angular style of architecture. New canopies were provided for both platforms at the time of rebuilding in the early 1930s. (Lens of Sutton)

77. This is the view from the footbridge as the decking nears completion. Until the rebuilding, London Transport had to operate the special RLH class low-bridge double deck buses on route 127. The crossover was used regularly during the engineering work shown in picture no. 28. (A.N.Davenport)

78. Class N no. 31857 and a policeman were in attendance as crowds climbed the footbridge to witness the unusual and impressive operation. (A.N.Davenport)

79. This picture from April 1995 makes an interesting comparison with no. 70, which was taken from a similar viewpoint. The goods yard, which once had a crane of 7½ tons capacity, was closed on 6th May 1963. (M.J.Stretton)

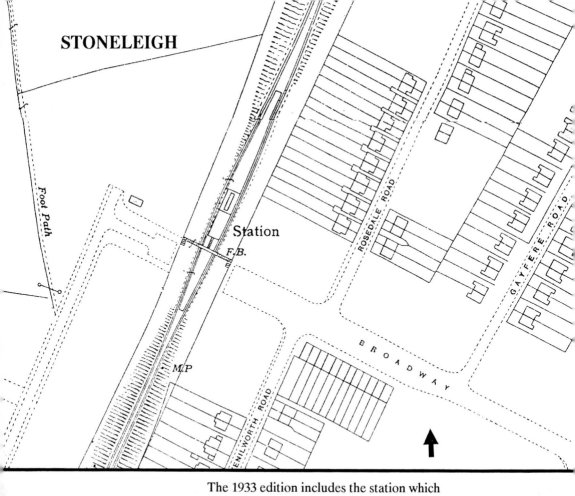

STONELEIGH

Foot Path

Station

F.B.

M.P.

KENILWORTH ROAD

ROSEDALE ROAD

GAYFERE ROAD

B R O A D W A Y

The 1933 edition includes the station which
opened on 17th July of the previous year.

80. A glance along the up side of the platform includes one of the automatic colour light intermediate block signals, which were in use from 1947 until 1966. (Lens of Sutton)

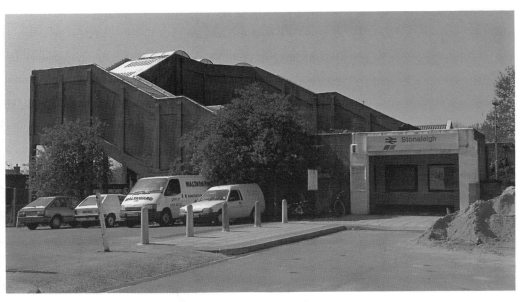

81.　The bridge shown on the map was re-placed by this structure which contained offices above the tracks. (M.Turvey)

82.　The small ticket office is included in this photograph of class 455 no. 5732 working the 11.04 Waterloo to Epsom on 2nd April 1995. The Network SouthEast nameboard had been replaced by the plain border style of South West Trains. (M.J.Stretton)

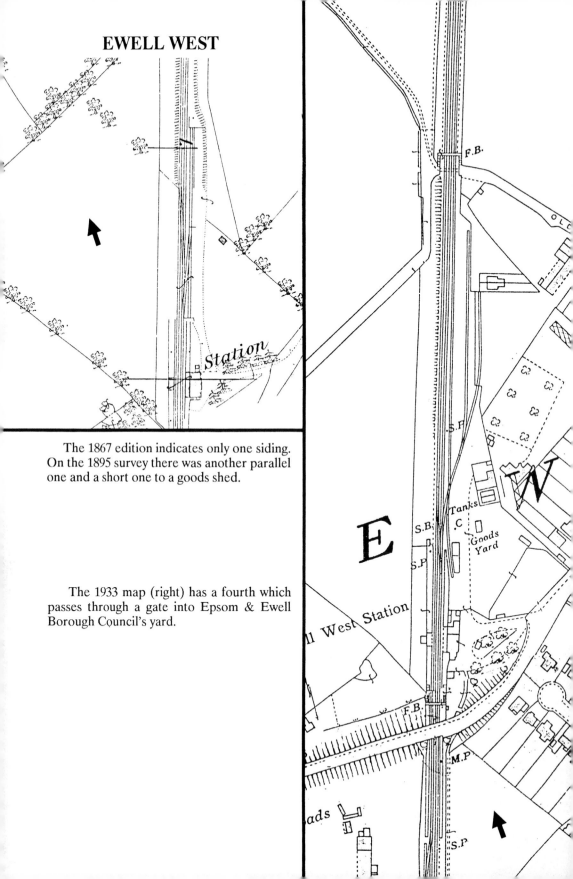

EWELL WEST

Station

The 1867 edition indicates only one siding. On the 1895 survey there was another parallel one and a short one to a goods shed.

The 1933 map (right) has a fourth which passes through a gate into Epsom & Ewell Borough Council's yard.

F.B.

S.F.

E

S.B.

S.P.

Tanks

C

Goods
Yard

W

ll West Station

F.B.

M.P.

ads

S.P.

83. The station opened with the line and was given the suffix "West" on 9th July 1923. Until that time it was known locally as "Ewell South Western". (Lens of Sutton)

84. The old established town had a biennial fair and a market every Thursday in the early part of the nineteenth century. This southward view shows the platforms continuing beyond the bridge and the connection to the Horton Light Railway near the ramps. (E.C.Bowden/P.D.McCann coll)

85. Its rural ambience survived into the era of the "Southern Electric". The population of Ewell grew from 2195 in 1861 to 4092 in 1901 and exploded after electrification. About ½ mile south of the station, a siding was provided on the down side in 1926 for the brickworks of Stone & Co. (Lens of Sutton)

86. The ground signal for the goods yard points and the goods shed are visible. The box of destination boards and the row of fire buckets are other items of a bygone age. (Lens of Sutton)

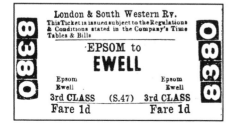

87. Class Q1 no. 33027 gave a rare sight of steam as it ran south on 22nd March 1964 with the LCGB/RCTS "Sussex Downsman" rail-tour. It proceeded to Guildford, Horsham, Hove, Three Bridges, East Grinstead, Tunbridge Wells West, Heathfield and Pevensey. It returned to London via the Kemp Town branch, Uckfield and Oxted. (J.Scrace)

88.   Although the goods yard closed on 1st May 1961, the goods shed was still standing to be photographed in February 1963. It was then used by a builders merchant and was subsequently demolished to make way for the inevitable car park. (P.Nicholson)

89.   The crane had been rated at 4 tons 11cwt and had a wooden jib. The signal box, photographed in June 1965, was closed on 27th February 1966. Note its unusual recess to accommodate the barrow crossing. (P.Nicholson)

90. Most suburban stations had at least one coal order office until the advent of the coal concentration depots and the closure of local yards. Wavy elm and herring-bone brickwork was intended to maintain the rural charm that was being lost as more semis were built. The building later became a taxi office.
(P.Nicholson)

91. A March 1990 photograph reveals that the station had retained most of its historic features, despite the surrounding urbanisation and the race for modernisation. One siding was so long that it passed under the footbridge in the distance until 1955. The up platform shelter was burnt down in October 1994.
(A.N.Davenport)

92. The narrow platforms under the bridge are less dangerous now that train doors are no longer hinged. Class 455 no. 5870 is braking as it approaches with the 10.50 Epsom to Waterloo service on 2nd April 1995.
(M.J.Stretton)

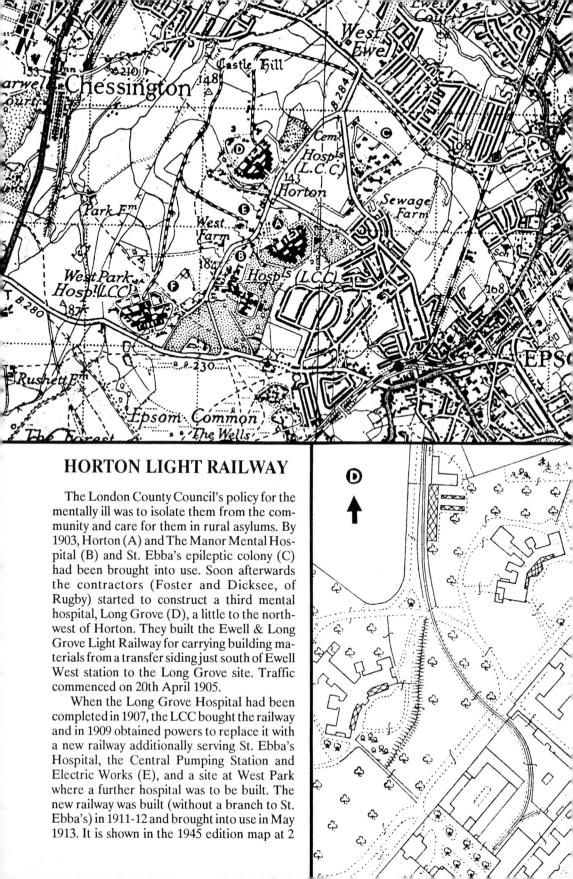

HORTON LIGHT RAILWAY

The London County Council's policy for the mentally ill was to isolate them from the community and care for them in rural asylums. By 1903, Horton (A) and The Manor Mental Hospital (B) and St. Ebba's epileptic colony (C) had been brought into use. Soon afterwards the contractors (Foster and Dicksee, of Rugby) started to construct a third mental hospital, Long Grove (D), a little to the northwest of Horton. They built the Ewell & Long Grove Light Railway for carrying building materials from a transfer siding just south of Ewell West station to the Long Grove site. Traffic commenced on 20th April 1905.

When the Long Grove Hospital had been completed in 1907, the LCC bought the railway and in 1909 obtained powers to replace it with a new railway additionally serving St. Ebba's Hospital, the Central Pumping Station and Electric Works (E), and a site at West Park where a further hospital was to be built. The new railway was built (without a branch to St. Ebba's) in 1911-12 and brought into use in May 1913. It is shown in the 1945 edition map at 2 ins to 1 mile and followed a route mostly to the north of the original line.

The building of West Park Hospital (F) was started in 1915 but delays due to World War I caused the work to continue until 1924. The HLR remained in use for taking coal to the various sites until closure in 1950.

D. Before reaching the boiler house at Long Grove Hospital, the line passed the glass-houses where coal could be unloaded. Traffic commenced to this site on 20th April 1905.

E Although described as "Pumping Station", the building housed the electricity generators and so this branch carried coal throughout the year. The engine shed is on the right. The area is known as "Sherwood".

F Shown near West Park Hospital is one of four loops on the system where wagons could be stored or run round. There were usually about 7000 patients in the group of hospitals and around 15000 tons of coal were required per annum.

E

Resr.

Chy.

Pumping Station
(London County Council)

F

F.B.

F.B.

WEST
PARK
HOSPITAL

Chy.

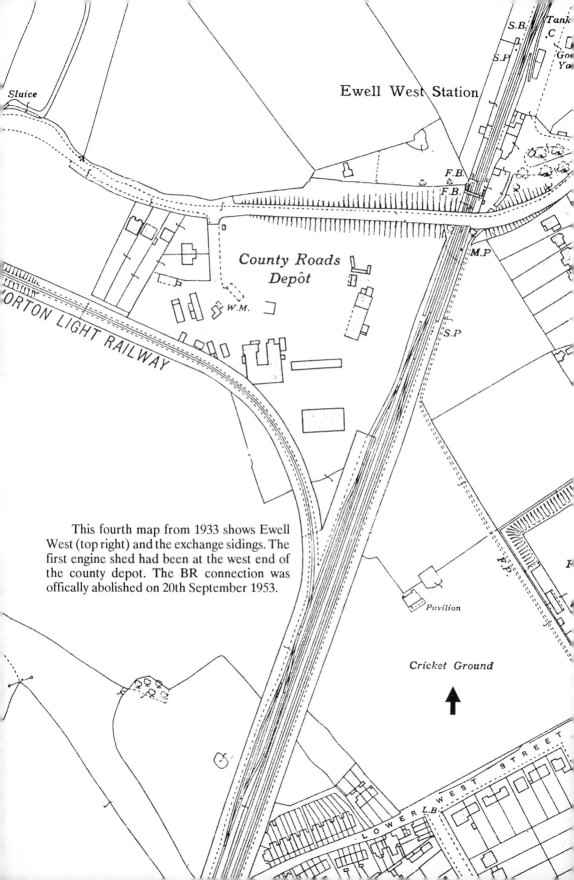

Sluice

Ewell West Station

S.B.   Tank

S.P.   C.

Go
Ya

F.B.

F.B.

M.P.

County Roads
Depôt

ORTON LIGHT RAILWAY

W.M.

S.P.

This fourth map from 1933 shows Ewell
West (top right) and the exchange sidings. The
first engine shed had been at the west end of
the county depot. The BR connection was
offically abolished on 20th September 1953.

F.P.

Pavilion

Cricket Ground

LOWER WEST STREET

L.B.

93.   The first locomotive was *Hollymoor*, a Manning Wardle 0-6-0ST. Andrew Barclay 0-4-0ST *Crossness* was in use until 1935, its maximum load being twelve wagons, except on the 1 in 40 gradient down to West Park where the limit was eight. This is its replacement *Hendon* which ran until 1947, having been built by Manning Wardle in 1926 with works no. 2046. (Pamlin Prints)

94.   This 0-4-0ST was built for the line in 1947 by Robert Stephenson & Hawthorns with works no. 7349 and is seen in the exchange sidings on 10th November of that year. The photographer confirms that the locomotive never carried a nameplate, although the name *Sherwood* has been attributed to it in several articles. The dumb-buffered 3-plank HLR wagon has its sides down, partly obscuring its timber frame.   (A.N.Davenport)

95. The railway closed in January 1950 and the exchange sidings were recorded in the following month. The gate and Ewell West station are in the distance. (D.Cullum)

96. The ELGLR crossed Hook Road on the level but a fatality in 1906 resulted in the HLR being provided with a bridge. The substantial structure is seen in 1950, when trespass and vandalism was becoming a problem. The arch now allows pedestrians access to Horton Country Park from a car park. (D.Cullum)

97. The line's last locomotive is running round loaded coal wagons on the loop near the junction between the Central Power Station and West Park lines on 29th December 1948. (A.N.Davenport)

———————▶

98. The locomotive shed, pictured in 1950, was situated on the approach to the Power Station. Weighted point levers were universal. P class 0-6-0T no. 1555 was hired from the SR for a period during 1938. (D.Cullum)

99.   The shed was photographed on 17th
October 1949 when the coal stage had been
inexplicably overfilled. Many boilerhouses
were supplied with narrow gauge skips for ash
removal. (A.N.Davenport)

100.   Dismantling was recorded on 26th March 1950, as was much of the HLR's wagon fleet. Light-weight rail had been used - hence the railway's name. It was not legally a "Light Railway" under the 1896 Act. The rail saw further use in Nigeria. (A.N.Davenport)

101. The footbridge on the path between Hook Road (Epsom) and Chessington Road (Ewell) was one of four over the railway, a generous provision with usually only one train per day. It was a necessary one in view of the number of mentally handicapped people perambulating locally. The bridge is being dismantled on 1st April 1950. (A.N.Davenport)

102. A short while later some parts of the bridge had been loaded onto a flat wagon. Devoid of its original sides, this was one of five ash wagons on the HLR. The locomotive was only three years old and was sold to a dealer. (A.N.Davenport)

103. A final look at this little known line shows part of the route parallel to the Chessington Road, shortly after closure. Passengers were never carried offically, although workmen were known to have travelled in wagons during the building work. Part of the route is now in the Horton Country Park and a circular walk is available to see some of the former railway sites. (D.Cullum)

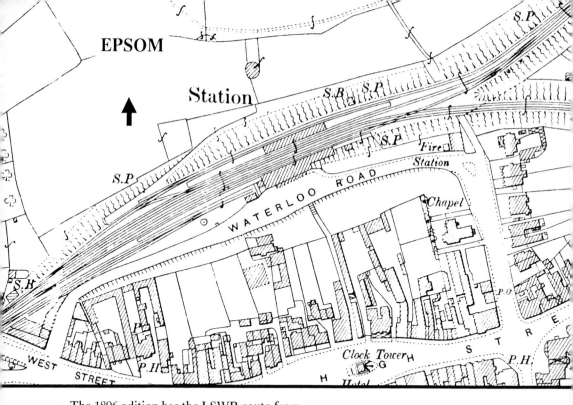

EPSOM

Station

S.P

WATERLOO ROAD

Fire Station

Chapel

S.H.

P.O

P.H.

WEST STREET

P II

Clock Tower

Hotel

STRE

H

The 1896 edition has the LSWR route from Wimbledon at the top, the LBSCR line from Sutton on the right and the joint railway to Leatherhead on the left. The LBSCR had its own station further east, its trains passing through this one on the centre roads shown.

104. A Waterloo-Guildford train crosses over the LBSCR tracks as it approaches the down platform. The signal post on the right carried an arm to start up trains on race days only. (P.D.McCann coll)

105. The cramped goods yard (centre) consisted of two sidings. There was also a very short dock siding (right), in which a horse box is standing. The yard closed on 3rd January 1928 when traffic was concentrated on the much larger ex-LBSCR depot at Epsom Town. (Lens of Sutton)

106. One of the two goods sidings is visible as the first electric train arrives on 9th July 1925. Public services to Waterloo commenced on the 12th. Note that the through lines had no conductor rails, as the line from Sutton was not electrified until March 1929. (P.D.McCann coll)

107.   Ex-SECR class R1 no. A706 speeds through with a London Bridge to Dorking North train on 2nd October 1926. The squat timber buildings probably dated from the opening of the line in 1859. (H.C.Casserley)

108.   Examination of the map will show that there was an up loop line. This is on the left of the picture, which was taken on 9th March 1929 during the rebuilding of the station. The ex-LSWR up main line had been removed by that time. (Late E.Wallis)

109. Looking in the other direction from a temporary footbridge, we see the two new island platforms, together with the new signal box which replaced those seen in pictures 105 and 108. The old vaulted roof of the up platform was soon to go. (H.C.Casserley)

110. The view towards Leatherhead from the signal box includes a number of ringed arm shunt signals. These allowed trains to run forward to reverse in the up or down electrified berthing sidings beyond the road bridge. This and the next three pictures were taken in 1930. (Railway Engineer)

111. The down Waterloo line swings in from the left while the Victoria lines curve right, between the two new luggage lifts. The signals are those seen in picture no. 108, the lower arm being a distant worked from Epsom Town box. (Railway Engineer)

112. The main entrance was to the left of the camera, the booking office being to the right. Access to the platforms was under the signs; a separate subway was provided for luggage, parcels, fish and milk. (Railway Engineer)

114. When opened, the words *EPSOM STA TION* were over the van yard of the parcels office. The letters were later moved to replace *SOUTHERN RAILWAY* over the main entrance. *British Rail Epsom* followed in due course. (Lens of Sutton)

115. The revised track layout is apparent on the illuminated diagram in this 1962 photograph. The 60-lever box closed on 29th July 1990. Only two ground signals were mechanically operated towards the end of its life. (A.N.Davenport)

113. Pound Lane had been designated a public footpath only and was widened greatly following the demolition of the small brick arch at the London end of the platforms. The new highway (named Waterloo Road) encouraged residential development north of the railway. (Railway Engineer)

116. The LSWR goods yard was redesigned in 1929 to have one long and one short siding for horse traffic. Assorted horse boxes and a bogie van were recorded at the special platform in September 1963. The platform was also useful for pre-Christmas mail traffic. (D.Clayton)

117. The up starting signals were replaced by colour lights in February 1966. The nearest semaphore post is of the LSWR lattice type while its neighbour was made by the SR from two running rails. (A.N.Davenport)

118. Three 4COR units were pictured on 2nd January 1972 on their way to Lancing after the final working of such stock on the South Western Division. After the electrification of the Victoria to Portsmouth service in 1938, such units passed non-stop through Epsom every hour. (R.E.Ruffell)

119. The roof of the box underwent extensive repairs in 1989, it having become a listed structure. Despite this, its demolition went ahead and is seen in progress on 4th March 1992. Provision of a footbridge over the down loop could have created a unique"des res". (A.N.Davenport)

Companion albums to feature
this station -
Epsom to Horsham
West Croydon to Epsom

120. The functional exterior was pictured in 1995 as it awaited a further change of lettering. By that time BR had been chopped into 167 portions - one hopes that the Beeching axe has not been resharpened. (M.J.Stretton)